PIRATE'S LOG LIGHT

Okay, pirates. This is the page all abc
pulls out of the spine of this book)
and a quote from a famous pirate a
because they made us, but the rea

How to work the light

- Turn light on by pulling it out of the spine until it clicks into place and
  the bulb lights.
- Turn light off by pushing it back into the spine.

Replacing the batteries

- The light uses two AAA batteries.
- When the light gets dim, it is time to replace the batteries.
- To remove the batteries, find the battery case at the bottom of the spine
  and unscrew the screw.
- Slide the battery case in the direction of the arrow.
- Remove the used batteries and insert two new ones (make sure the poles
  are correctly oriented).
- Slide battery door back in until it clicks into place and reinstall the screw.

**"Yarr, I use my book light to check myself for ticks. Sea-ticks."
—Long John Silver, on his 51st birthday**

Warning

- The light is meant to turn only from side to side. Do not twist it all the
  way around.
- When replacing batteries, do not mix new batteries with batteries that
  have already been used. Do not mix alkaline, standard (carbon-zinc), or
  rechargeable (nickel-cadmium).
- Replace any battery that leaks with a new one.
- If you do not plan to use the light for a month or longer, remove the
  batteries from the battery case.
- Please discard used batteries at official collection sites in cooperation
  with national or local regulations.

What did we tell you ? The fun is on the *next* page. And the page after that.
Then a few stinkers. But then fun again! Then a sea-tick. So turn the page
already!

Design by Jessica Dacher.
Typeset in Agenda and Kennel District.
Manufactured in China.
ISBN 978-0-8118-6435-0

Chronicle Books endeavors to use environmentally
responsible paper in its gift and stationery products.

10 9 8 7 6 5 4 3 2 1

Chronicle Books LLC
680 Second Street
San Francisco, California 94107

www.chroniclebooks.com

PIRATE'S LOG

A HANDBOOK FOR ASPIRING SWASHBUCKLERS

by **JORY JOHN AND AVERY MONSEN**
illustrated by **GILBERT FORD**

chronicle books · san francisco

hello there

This is the first page in *Pirate's Log*, your brand-new pirate jaarrrrnal. (Yeah, we know it's usually spelled "journal," but try saying it our way, out loud, right now, wherever you are: *Jarrrrrnal!* Good. Try it again, with a little more rasp in your voice: *Jaarrrrrrrrrrrrrnal!!* Even better. See how much more fun it is this way? See how many people turned around and stared at you? Get used to it. Pirates don't care when people turn and stare at them. That was your **FIRST IMPORTANT LESSON**.)

When you're finished with this *jaaaaaaaaaaaaarrrrrrrrrnal!!!*, you'll most likely be putting the *Arrr* sound into everything, almost to the point where it's annoying. Here are a few more words where *Arrr* would fit in comfortably:

1. Arrrctic
2. Monkey barrrrrs
3. Harry Parrrrrtarrrrr and the Prisonarrrrrr of Arrrrrzkabarrrrrn

Go ahead and say all three of those now. Are people looking at you again? **GOOD**.

So here's how to use this *jaaaaaaaaaaaaaaarrrrrrrrrrrrrrrrrrrrnal!!!!*
The book contains a bunch of instructions for games and

challenges and fun writing activities. Each completed page will get you one step closer to becoming a full-fledged, parrot-wearing, seafaring, boat-steering pirate!

There is a list of pirate-rankings on page 172. We'll let you know when it's okay to check a box off and improve your standing. For now, you're going to be known as **SHARK-BAIT**, Shark-Bait, so you should go to page 172 and check that name. (You'll want to improve on this ranking quickly. Especially when there's a shark nearby and people are looking for some bait to catch it with!)

Remember this, Shark-Bait: pirating is not as easy as it looks. For instance, you think that "X" always marks the spot? Well . . . sometimes it's just an "X." Tricky, huh?

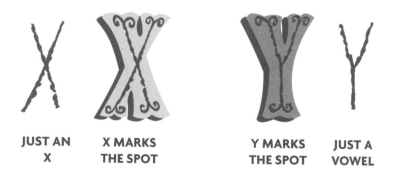

| JUST AN X | X MARKS THE SPOT | Y MARKS THE SPOT | JUST A VOWEL |

And sometimes "Y" marks the spot, simply to throw you off the trail. And sometimes "Y" is a vowel, but we're not going to try to explain that one here.

We're sure you've noticed that there's a neat light in the spine of this book. Check it out. Flip it on and off. Go to town on that thing. It's going to come in handy. See, most of the writing you're doing should and will take place when the sun goes down and the lights are off. Pirates prefer it this way, with no one bothering them by looking over their shoulder except, maybe, a nosy parrot.

So before you begin, do you have any questions? Anything at all? Just kidding. We can't hear you. And we're making most of this up as we go along, anyway. That was your **SECOND IMPORTANT LESSON**. The lesson was: We're making this up. And so should you! That's the best part of the *Pirate's Log*. You can write whatever you want in here, whether it's true or false or serious or ridiculous. If you want to read a bunch of historical pirate facts, you've got the wrong book. But if you're ready to set sail on your journey to actually becoming a pirate, turn to the next page, Shark-Bait. Your crew is waiting for you.

Keep your eyes open for the **VERY IMPORTANT LESSONS** contained throughout (you've already heard two) and enjoy your *jaaaaaaaaaaaaaaaaaaaaaarrrrrrrrrrrrrrrrrrrrrrrrrrrrnal!!!!!!!!*

Your friends,
Avery & Jory *(The guys who wrote this stuff and who know a whole lot about becoming pirates.)*

CHOOSE YOUR PIRATE NAME

First things first, **SHARK-BAIT**: Let's figure out your pirate name! After all, if you walk onto a pirate ship with a name like Sammy or Doug, it's quite possible you'll be walking the plank within minutes. (No offense, Sammies and Dougs.) Whatever your name happens to be right now, you'll need something a little different if you're going to be a real buccaneer.

We think that one of the best pirate names is Long John Silver. Say it out loud. It's got a nice ring to it, huh?

Well, using our Pirate Name Formula (or, PNF), you can have a name just as cool as ol' Long John. Here's all you need to do. Fill these out:

Descriptive Word + Name + Something Shiny =
Your Pirate Name!

Simple enough, right? Now you try:

- - - - - - - - - - - - - - - - - + - - - - - - - - - - - - - - - - - + - - - - - - - - - - - - - - - - =

- -

If you want, you can try a bunch of different versions:

---------------+---------------+---------------=

---------------+---------------+---------------=

---------------+---------------+---------------=

---------------+---------------+---------------=

Final Pirate Name:

---------------+---------------+---------------=

Don't you feel more dangerous now?

Way **MORE DANGEROUS** and *way* **MORE SHINY**.

Here's a few we came up with:

OLD WALTER GOLDENTOOTH
STINKY STEVE RHINESTONES
DANCIN' JACK SILVERSNATCHER
PRANCIN' SIMON BRONZEBREATH
JOLLY JULIE KIDNEYSTONE
BONY TONY BALONEY
GRUMBLIN' ARTHUR PLATINUM-PANTS
CRANKY MICKEY METAL-BUM

(We know baloney isn't shiny, and we know that it's supposed to be spelled bologna, but it's our book and we can do what we want, especially when it comes to sandwich meats and spelling.)

Now that you've got a name, you've got to practice your pirate autograph. When you're the world's most famous pirate, and people are coming up to you all the time and they're like, "Hey you! You world-famous sea adventurer! Can I have your autograph?!" you're going to have to be ready to sign. So get prepared here and figure out the best way to write your pirate name. Try it all swoooooshy and try it all stiff. Try it in cursive, if you can. In fact, how many signatures can you fit on this page? Write the total in the corner.

YARR,
CAN I HAVE YOUR
AUTOGRAPH? AND
SOME BALONEY
IF YOU'VE GOT IT?

- - - - - - - - - - - -

total signatures

CHOOSING YOUR SHIP'S NAME

You're going to be sailing for a good long time, and it's important to have a ship name that you like and respect. The captain's in a good mood today, and he's going to let you suggest a name for the ship for the duration of your adventure. The only rule: the word *The* has to appear before whatever words you choose. It just sounds cooler that way. Here are some examples:

THE QUEEN MARY
THE SEA DOG
THE LOST CAUSE
THE BEES KNEES
THE TOOTH FERRY
THE PINK EYE
THE BRITISH INVASION
THE HEARTY STEW
THE DINGY DINGHY
THE SITTING DUCK
THE TOM CRUISELINER

* Wait a minute. These sound like awesome band names. Except The Pink Eye. That band sounds itchy and contagious.

Now you try:

The _____ _____

The _____ _____

The _____ _____

The _____ _____

The _____ _____

The _____ _____

The _____ _____

The _____ _____

The _____ _____

Your ship's final name:

The _____ _____

PACK YOUR STUFF

If you complete all the challenges in this book, you just might become a real pirate. Then you'll be sailing the seas for who knows how long. We don't know. You don't know. Nobody knows. Anyway, look around your room and pick the ten things that you're going to bring with you. We know what you're thinking: "Maybe I'll bring eleven things." But you can't, **SHARK-BAIT**. The last guy who brought eleven things had to walk eleven planks! He's still alive, but he's not very happy about how wet he got. It ruined a really nice pair of pants, and he was pretty embarrassed. That's your **THIRD IMPORTANT LESSON**.

Now list the things you're bringing:

1. ---

2. ---

3. ---

4. ---

5. ---

6.- -

7.- -

8.- -

9.- -

10.- -

11.- -

WHAT DID WE TELL YOU ABOUT ELEVEN?

orion

Little Dipper

Big Dipper

LOOK AT thE STARS

It's time to get some use out of the nifty light that's attached to this book, if you haven't already!

Pirates use the stars to guide them when sailing at night — constellations like Orion, the Little Dipper, and the Big Dipper.

Turn out the lights in your room, turn on the book light, and connect the dots on this page and the next one to make some constellations of your own. Make them creative and give them catchy names. We've used the same darn constellations for so long. It'll be a welcome relief to have some new ones!

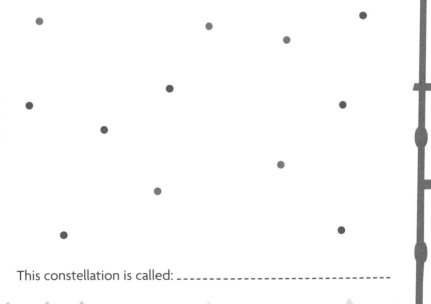

This constellation is called: _

This constellation is called: _____

This constellation is called: _____

⚓ THE KNOT-TYING CHALLENGE

Any captain can tell you that the most important skill on a pirate ship is knot-tying. This is your **FOURTH IMPORTANT LESSON**. One famous pirate, Grimy Pete Copperbottom, accidentally tied his ship to a dock with a *slipknot*. Bad move, Copperbottom. His boat came untied within minutes and drifted out to sea while Copperbottom was on land buying snacks. The moral of the story is: Pirates love snacks. The second moral of the story is: Pirates need to know how to tie knots. Got it? Good.

What you'll need for this challenge: One pair of shoes with laces. One stopwatch. If you don't have a stopwatch, you can just get a friend to count to sixty slowly. If your friend can't count to sixty, go buy a stopwatch and then find a math tutor for your friend.

Here's how to do this challenge: See how many times you can tie and untie your shoes in a minute. Check out our official Knot-Tying Ranking System:

1–3 times: Fumbly-fingers
4–6 times: Average
7–9 times: Pretty darned good
10 and above: The Lace-Master!

RANKING ALERT!
Congratulations on getting through your first Pirate Challenge! You may flip to page 172 and put a check next to LANDLUBBER, because that's your new status, Landlubber.

YOUR EYE PATCH

Okay. Let's talk eye patches, **LANDLUBBER**! Every pirate who's any pirate wears a patch over at least one of his or her eyes, most of the time. This is your **FIFTH IMPORTANT LESSON**. Use this handy chart to figure out which of your eyes is still working.

Directions: Set this book on one side of your bed. Cover one eye with your hand. Stick out your tongue. Say "ahhh." Good. Everything looks fine so far. You can put your tongue back in your mouth. Now, read as far as you can with one eye, and then repeat with the other. We take this test very seriously. We hope you will, too.

ONCE UPON A TIME
THERE WAS AN EYE TEST
HAPPENING ON SOME KID'S BED
SOMEWHERE. THE BED WAS PRETTY
MESSY AND SMELLED KINDA FUNNY. BUT

WHO ARE WE KIDDING? THERE'S NO WAY YOUR EYES ARE GOOD

ENOUGH TO READ THIS FAR, ANYWAY. WE COULD SAY ANYTHING HERE,

BLAH BLAH BLEE BLAH. ARRRRRRRRRRR.

Now that you've taken the test, fill out the following information. You'll be wearing your patch over the weaker eye. Or the stronger eye, if you're crazy. Or both, if you don't mind walking into a wall.

Stronger eye *(circle one):*

    Left / Right

Weaker eye *(circle one):*

    Left / Right

 THE EYE-PATCH CHALLENGE

Now that you know which eye you're going to cover up, you're ready for an eye patch, right? Wrong! If you get an eye patch without preparing for it, you're likely to get laughed off the ship and into the ocean and *right into the belly of a shark!* This is your **SIXTH IMPORTANT LESSON**: You gotta *earn* your patch, Landlubber. In this challenge, you'll get one step closer.

What you'll need for this challenge: Eyes (at least one). Eyelids (same amount).

Here's how to do this challenge: Close one eye.

Either one will work. Got it?

Right or left eye: --

Okay, now keep it closed all day.

What? You've given up already? Okay, so maybe it won't be an all-day thing, but let's keep that eye closed for a little while, while we try to do some stuff.

.

Here are some activities we recommend trying with one eye closed (check them off after you've done them).

☐ Tying your shoes
☐ Tying somebody else's shoes
☐ Walking (slowly) from room to room
☐ Washing the dishes
☐ Playing Ping-Pong* (See bottom of page for a pirate Ping-Pong rumor.)
☐ Walking on your tiptoes along a straight line while juggling and humming and thinking about math

Here are some things you should not do with one eye closed (check them off when you do not do them).

☐ Working with power tools
☐ Walking a tightrope
☐ Piloting a helicopter

* We hear Blackbeard had an impressive backhand slam!

Write down some things that were tricky to do with one eye closed: ---

----

ALL RIGHT! If you completed this challenge, you can flip to page 172 and check off Squid-Kisser. Because that's what you are now, SQUID-KISSER. Nice work! No more landlubbing for you! If any squid need kissing, you'll be the first one called upon! What an honor!

Here's your eye patch, **SQUID-KISSER**. Cut it out along the dotted line, and punch two holes in it. Thread a piece of string through those holes and tie it around your head. Bam! You've got yourself a genuine eye patch! (If you wear glasses, you can just wear the patch under your glasses.)

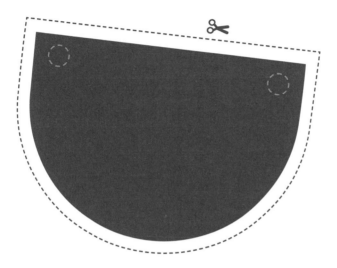

Wear your eye patch around for a day. How did people react? Did it help you make any new friends? Well, that's just fine, Squid-Kisser, because pirates need friends like a fish needs a bicycle. (They don't. Unless we're talking about some sort of superfish. Or a bicycle somehow built for undersea commuting.)

HOW MANY PIRATES?

In battle, it's important to know what you're up against. Quick estimations can make all the difference between a long life of luxury and an untimely end of shame. Even in times of peace this is important to know, for different reasons altogether, which we won't go into here.

Take a quick ten-second glance at the next page, which is full of tiny pirates (they're tiny because, right now, they're far away). Then turn back to this page.

YOU'RE BACK?

Okay. Now (without looking again or counting) you're going to estimate the number of pirates on the page.

Write your answer here: I'm going to say that there are around

--------------- pirates.

After you've guessed, turn to page 31.

You'll find the correct number of pirates at the very bottom of the page.

How many pirates were you off by? - - - - - - - - - - - - - - -

If you were off by more than **1,000 PiRATeS**, you might want to stay below deck when trouble's brewing.

If you were off by more than **500 PiRATeS**, there's a chance this battle thing wouldn't work out for you, and maybe you should stick to the cooking or cleaning or some behind-the-scenes work.

If you missed it by **100 PiRATeS**, we're impressed. This was a tricky guess, and you did well. But don't get full of yourself. You're still a squid-kisser, Squid-Kisser.

If you missed it by **50 OR FeWeR PiRATeS**, you might be captain material after all! We've got our one good eye on you.

There are 143 pirates.

⚓ THE SCURVY-PREVENTION CHALLENGE

Being on a ship for long periods of time means it's hard to get fresh fruit, even if you really want some. There's not much room for a lime tree on that deck, and if there were, some pirate would probably cut it down to make a peg leg and use the limes in some sort of battle.

Because pirates can't easily find fresh citrus fruit, they often get a disease called scurvy. This is your **SEVENTH IMPORTANT LESSON** and today, you'll be avoiding scurvy at all costs. At all costs, **SQUID-KISSER!**

What you'll need for this challenge: A bunch of fruit. It's probably in your kitchen. Go check. Got some? Good. (If not, request a special trip to the store. When you say it's for some fruit, your folks will probably jump at the chance!)

Here's how to do this challenge: For dinner, ask for a fruit salad the size of your head. Eat as much as you can, but take it slow. If somebody asks you why you want so much fruit, show them this diagram:

FRUIT FOR
DINNER

NO FRUIT
FOR DINNER

List the all the different fruits you managed to eat:

Once you've eaten your fruit and written
about it and drawn a picture of it mashed
up in your belly, you can turn to page 172.
Guess what! You can stop kissing all those
squid and check off the box next to your
new title: PARROT-TRAINER! Wow!
What a quick rise in ranking!

Now draw what the chewed-up fruit looks like in your stomach (this should be gross, **SQUID-KISSER**):

⚓ THE HOOK-FINGER CHALLENGE

A lot of pirates have hooks because, one way or another, they lost a hand or two, or—much more rarely—three. It's just another part of daily life at sea. This is your **EIGHTH IMPORTANT LESSON**. So for this challenge, **PARROT-TRAINER**, you're going to experience what it was like for our hook-wearing brothers and sisters.

What you'll need for this challenge: At least one pointer finger. Got one? Go ahead and choose it now. We'll wait.

Right or left pointer finger: _____

Here's how to do this challenge: Find a clock before you start. Figure out what time it is. Write down the time you see here: _____ : _____ a.m. / p.m. *(circle one)*

Now make a fist. Stick out a pointer finger (fig. 1) and bend it so it looks like a hook (fig. 2).

This is what we will call "Hook-Finger Position." Get used to it. (If you're feeling *really* brave, try it with *both* pointer fingers.) Now we're going to see just how long you can do this.

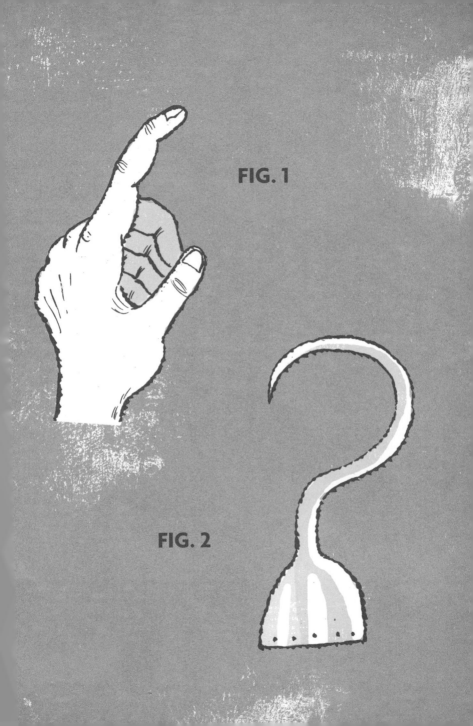

FIG. 1

FIG. 2

Here are a few fun things to try, once you've got your hooks up and running. Check these activities off as you do them:

☐ Writing in this journal *(see the next page)*
☐ Nose-picking
☐ Remote-control controlling
☐ Typing on your computer
☐ Playing video games
☐ Pointing at yourself

Are you finished already? Fine. Write your ending time here:

_____ : _____ a.m. / p.m. *(circle one)*

Write the total amount of time you were in hook-finger position here: _____ : _____ (If you think you can do it better, try again. Seriously, we'll wait.)

What was the hardest thing to accomplish with your hooks?

Write it here: _____
_____
_____

Could you live with hooks forever if you had to? *(circle one)*

a. Maybe.   b. Maybe not.   c. It depends.

While holding a pencil in your "hook," write a short story about a boy or girl who—all of a sudden—had hooks for fingers. Try not to make the handwriting too sloppy. And good luck.

Here are some questions to get you started: What kind of challenges does our character face? How do people treat him or her at school? What are the good things about having hooks for fingers? What is the boy or girl's greatest wish? How did he or she happen to have hook fingers to begin with?

If you made it through the Hook-Finger Challenge without getting a serious hand cramp, you can flip to page 172 and change your status to SPIT-SCRUBBER. Hooray! What's that? You say you'd rather hang out with parrots than scrub pirate-loogies off the deck? Too bad, Spit-Scrubber. It's scrubbin' time.

HOOK ALTERNATIVES

Everybody knows a pirate's favorite hand-replacement is a hook. Hooks are great for popping balloons and spearing fish and waving at your enemies. But today's pirate can use just about anything to replace a lost hand. Here we have a few pirates who are missing their hands. Draw anything other than a hook on them, and give them each a funny name. We'll give you an example:

CAPTAIN ARCHIBALD SANDWICH-HAND

YOUR UGLY FACE

Pirates are usually pretty ugly. Much uglier than you or I. And we don't know *why* they're so ugly. But if you want to see what you'll look like after a couple years at sea, try this: At night, turn out all the lights in your room except for the light attached to this book. Go stand in front of a mirror. Hold the book light underneath your chin, shining it up toward your face. Now squish your face up like you've just taken a big bite of a lemon. Ugly, right? Yeah. Real ugly. Now, try moving the light around and scrunching up your face in different ways. Even uglier! Wow, that's really ugly. For all of our sakes, try to avoid that from now on. Instead, draw in the mirror below. Try not to scare yourself.

Goodness, you're going to make a **GREAT** pirate!

⚓ THE SHAVING CHALLENGE

It's tremendously hard to shave when you're out at sea. With that ship bobbing up and down in those unpredictable ocean waves, there is a good chance of getting nicks and cuts. And that's the last thing anybody wants. That was your **NINTH IMPORTANT LESSON**.

So this week—boy or girl, young or old—you're going to go without shaving! Pirates did it, so you'll have to, as well!

What you'll need for this challenge: A face. A week.

Here's how to do this challenge: No matter how hard it seems, you simply must not shave for the next seven days. That's right Seven. Days. Got it? Okay, go!

Wait, you've given up already? You've already shaved since you read those last few sentences?

Come on! How hard could this possibly be?

Let's start again, and this time for real. Repeat after us: "No. Shaving. Arrr."

Here's what we think you'll look like throughout the week:

1. MONDAY

2. TUESDAY

3. WEDNESDAY

4. THURSDAY

5. FRiDAY

6. SATURDAY

7. SUNDAY

Here are some activities we recommend you do while trying not to shave:

☐ Looking in the mirror

☐ Talking about shaving

☐ Talking about not shaving

☐ Talking about mirrors

In fact, anything but the actual act of shaving is all right with us!

Now draw seven pictures of yourself in the boxes provided below, each detailing exactly how much facial hair you have grown, day-by-day. How accurate were our drawings of you, **SPIT-SCRUBBER**?

1. MONDAY

2. TUESDAY

3. WEDNESDAY

4. THURSDAY

5. FRIDAY

6. SATURDAY

7. SUNDAY

CONGRATULATIONS!
You've passed from Spit-Scrubber to MOP-CARRIER. Go wash your hands, and then check the Mop-Carrier box on page 172.

the PeOPLe YOU KNOW

We know you have a bunch of people in your life you see every single day, whether you want to or not, from your teachers to your parents to your classmates to the lunch lady and the guy who drives the school bus.

Take a moment to think about all those people. Now fill in the blanks.

Who looks the most like a pirate? _____
_____
_____

Who looks the least like a pirate? _____
_____
_____

Who smells like a pirate? _____
_____
_____

Who sounds like a pirate? _____
_____
_____

Who probably secretly loves pirates? _____
_____
_____
_____

Who probably secretly despises pirates? _____
_____
_____
_____
_____

Which five people (whom you already know) would you like to
sail the seas with? _____
_____
_____
_____
_____

Which five people (whom you already know) would you never
want to sail with? _____
_____
_____
_____
_____

⚓ THE DAY-WITHOUT-A-BATH CHALLENGE

This one might need a little bit of permission. (So after you read this, go and ask if it's all right. It probably will be, but maybe it won't. If it's not, then you can skip ahead and do one of the other challenges in this book *twice* to make up for it.)

It's important to remember that sometimes, for months and months at sea, pirates don't take a bath! On the high seas, everybody has dirty bodies, *all the time!* This is your **TENTH IMPORTANT LESSON**.

What you'll need for this challenge: A body.

Here's how to do this challenge: For an entire day—morning, noon, and night—you'll need to avoid all types of baths and showers and any sort of water that would make you even the slightest bit cleaner.

This challenge is a fantastic and realistic way to see how pirates really smelled! For the full experience, remember to take huge whiffs of yourself throughout the day.

Also, it's important to tell at least five people that you're avoiding baths today and gauge their reactions. Report your findings below.

These are the five people I told I wasn't bathing today:

1. --

2. --

3. --

4. --

5. --

This is how I felt about myself: -----------------------------------

----

This is how many times I got really itchy: -----------------------

When I breathed in, I smelled exactly like ---------- -week-old
                                              (number)

   (type of food)

As soon as the day is over, go wash off. You're starting to attract flies, **MOP-CARRIER**!

Because you did such a good job at staying dirty, you can go to page 172 and check off SAILMAKER. You're moving up! But you do need to take a bath. Seriously.

YOUR FAVORITE FOOT

What are some words you would use to describe your foot? Soft? Ticklish? Smelly? Rotting? Footy? Well, a lot of pirates might use the word *missing* to describe one of their feet. That's just part of the pirate life, and it's your **ELEVENTH IMPORTANT LESSON**. The peg leg is an acceptable replacement, but it'll never be quite the same as a real foot.

Trace your foot on the next page. What are some things you'd like to remember about it? What are some fun things you did with it? Any rowdy races run? Any huge hills hiked? Any soccer goals scored? Tell us all about them: _____

_____

_____

_____

_____

_____

_____

_____

_____

_____

_____

Trace your foot here:

⚓ THE WOODEN-LEG CHALLENGE

We're not going to go into all the details here, but some pirates have only one working leg.

The other leg (the "peg leg") is often made out of wood or metal or pegs or who knows what . . . it's hard to say without doing the proper research, which usually takes a lot of time and is very tiring.

Anyway, today, you're going to pretend that you lost a leg. You can make up the "How I Lost It" story, whether it's shark-related, whale-related, tractor-related, or whatever. But it's good to have a few words ready, in case grown-ups ask you what you're doing. Some people might call this a lie, but we call it a More Interesting Version of the Truth (or MIVOTT).

Write a reason why you're missing a leg here: - - - - - - - - - - - - - - - -
- -

That sounds phony. Write a better reason here: - - - - - - - - - - - - -
- -

That's much better.

Here's how to do this challenge: Lock your knee and make one leg stiff as a board. Make the other one as loose as a goose. A sea goose!* (For more information on the sea goose—which we've just made up—see the bottom of this page.)

Now practice your limp in your bedroom. Back and forth, back and forth. Back. And. Forth. Good. Take your time and perfect your hobble and wobble. It helps if there's a mirror nearby. Are you hobbling and wobbling perfectly yet?

Now: Go out and take the world by storm, **SAILMAKER**! A *limping* storm! (If you happen to see somebody else taking the world by limping storm, chances are, they're reading this book too. You can nod your approval in their general direction.)

Spend today walking like this. Turn the page only after you've completed this activity.

*With proper nutrition, the sea goose can grow up to 200 feet long. If you lined up its feathers in a straight feathery line, it could reach from here to the sun! We think this is very, very impressive, even if it's false information. The sun is very hot.

WOW. We can't believe you spent the entire day walking like you had a wooden leg. We're seriously impressed. So impressed, in fact, that we've decided to upgrade you from Sailmaker to DECK-SWABBER. Check it off on page 172.

Draw the sea goose's feathers extending from Earth to the sun. Don't forget to draw some aliens and black holes and stuff. And some stink lines.

NiGht WRite

The open ocean can get pretty dark at night. When there's nothing but the moon and stars to light your way, performing your pirate duties (and your pirate doodies) can get really tricky. So let's see how good your night vision is. Wait until nighttime, when it's totally dark outside. Turn out the lights in your bedroom. If it's still light, you can get under your covers. Now turn on the light attached to this book and read the sentence below.

Shiver me timbers

Now, turn out the book light and try to copy the sentence exactly. Make it look exactly like the one above, if you can.

How well did you do? *(circle one)*

1. Okay.
2. Not very okay.
3. Less than not very okay.

Rent, Watch & Write

Before you go out and buy a parrot and tear up all your pants and quit bathing, let's make sure you really want to be a pirate. There are plenty of movies you can watch for a good hard look at the pirate lifestyle. Here are a few of our favorites:

THE PRINCESS BRIDE
MUPPET TREASURE ISLAND
PIRATES OF THE CARIBBEAN
YOU'VE GOT MAIL (UNRELATED, BUT STILL GOOD)
HOOK

Ask your parents to rent one of these movies. (A couple of them are PG-13, so make sure that's okay. One of them stars Tom Hanks, so make sure *that's* okay.) After you've watched it, write a little review.

What were your favorite parts? _
_ _
_ _
_ _
_ _
_ _

What were your least favorite parts? --------------------------
----

Would you have liked to be one of the pirates in the movie?
☐ Maybe
☐ Maybe not
☐ It depends

Is Tom Hanks everything he's cracked up to be?
☐ Oh yeah
☐ Oh no
☐ Why are you guys so interested in Tom Hanks?

Did you see *The Da Vinci Code*? What a jumbled mess,

Right?

tO BRiNg OR NOt tO BRiNg

On page 16, you listed some things you might bring with you on your journey. Here are a few things you are encouraged to bring:

(Check the box if you have these)

☐ Striped shirts

☐ A parrot or parrot substitute (a dove or a bat, perhaps?)

☐ A sense of adventure

☐ Pants that are torn at the bottom

☐ Regular pants (The crew may go out to dinner, and it's important that everyone looks nice.)

☐ A sense of humor

☐ A multivitamin

☐ A willingness to eat things that are gross (including rats)

A few things you are encouraged NOT to bring on a pirate ship:

(Check the box if you promise not to bring these)

☐ Polka-dotted shirts

☐ Sharks

☐ A crying baby

☐ Math textbooks

☐ A sense of smell

☐ Vampires

☐ Baby sharks

☐ Crying baby sharks

⚓ THE SEASICKNESS CHALLENGE

Have you ever been on a boat? Or on a long car ride? And have you ever gotten that oogley-googley-something's-just-not-right feeling in the pit of your stomach from all that rocking and rolling? Pirates spend most of their lives on boats, so they have to get used to seasickness. This is your **TWELFTH IMPORTANT LESSON**. In this challenge, you can feel all the dizziness and tummy-ache of the open ocean without ever leaving dry land!

What you'll need for this challenge: An open space with nothing fragile or breakable or sharp nearby. We recommend your front lawn, unless that's where you keep your steak knives and fine china.

Here's how to do this challenge: First, write your pirate name on the line below:

Good. Now, go find a nice safe spot, take a deep breath, and spin around ten times. Fast. Come on. You call that fast? My *grandma* could spin faster than that, and she was *never* a pirate!*

* Just kidding. We have no idea how fast you're spinning. We were just trying to rile you up.

After you've spun, sit back down and immediately write your pirate name again, right here:

Compare the two. Any noticeable differences? Is one *swooshier* than the other? Don't worry, that's normal.

Give it a few minutes, take a few breaths, and then spin ten times again. Got your sea legs? Good. Write your pirate name again, here:

(NOTE: If you start to feel sick, stop spinning. And whatever you do, **DON'T THROW UP ON THIS BOOK**. You'll be demoted AND your book will smell awful. Gross.)

As long as you didn't throw up on the book, you can go to page 172 and move on up to HOOK-SHARPENER. Nice job, pally. If you DID throw up on the book, figure out how to un-check all the boxes. Guess what: You're Shark-Bait again.

YOUR VERY OWN SHIP

One of the best parts about becoming a captain is getting your
own ship. When that time comes for you, what kind of ship do
you want?

Start by answering these questions and then go from there:
What will your ship be made of? Who else will be on board?
What special functions will your ship have? For instance, will it
be able to fly? Go underwater? Hop on land? Will there be an
onboard ice-cream store? What else will you see? A Starbucks?
Those things are everywhere!

Add any details that will make your ship original and different
from everybody else's! You want the most unique ship
imaginable! ---

⚓ THE SEAWATER CHALLENGE

What you'll need for this challenge: Some salt. Some water. A cup.

Here's how to do this challenge: Take a hearty five pinches of table salt and add it to the cup. Fill the cup with water. You're out at sea, **HOOK-SHARPENER**, so you're going to have to get used to the smell and taste and feel of salt water.

Take a whiff of your salt creation. Smells like the ocean, huh? (For an extra yuck factor, add a piece of fish to the mix!) Then gargle with your salty (maybe fishy) liquid. This means that you're going to swish the ocean around in your mouth! Gross. Can you taste that? Right now, you're tasting genuine *pirate life!*

What does pirate life taste and smell like? Is it awful? Kind of appetizing? Write about it here: _____
_____
_____

_____

_____

_____

_____

After you write a few sentences about your salty concoction, you can turn to page 172 and advance to the position of CARPENTER.

X MARKS THE SPOT

TRY PUTTING THIS IN YOUR FRONT YARD
TO SEE IF ANYBODY COMES AND DIGS A HOLE IN
THE GROUND, LOOKING FOR TREASURE.

FAMOUS PiRATE FLAGS

Here are a few famous pirate flags:

JOLLY ROGER

ONE-EYED JACK

STEDE BONNET'S
THE GENTLEMAN
PIRATE

THOMAS TEW'S
JOLLY ROGER

NEAt, huh?

Now it's your turn to make something neat.

YOUR OFFICIAL FLAG

The rectangle below is going to be your flag. But you have to make it your own. Here's how: Take a look at the symbols below and on the next page. Choose the three that represent you best, or invent some new ones. Draw them in the rectangle. Make sure you use a pencil first, in case you mess it up.

VOILA! YOUR VERY OWN PIRATE FLAG!

A SKULL & CROSSBONES
This means "Fear me, for I am dangerous"

A SANDWICH
This means "Fear me, for I am hungry and will eat all your sandwiches"

A PICTURE OF THIS BOOK
This means "Fear me, for I own a pirate journal"

A CELL PHONE
This means "Fear me, for I talk loudly in public places"

A FEATHER
This means "Fear me, for I will tickle when necessary"

A PILLOW
This means "Fear me, for I am sleepy"

A BAR OF SOAP
This means "Fear me, for I'm in need of a bath"

ASPIRIN
This means "Fear me, for I will cause a headache"

BANJO
This means "Fear me, for I will play the banjo"

A QUARTER
This means, "Fear me, for I will ask to borrow a quarter and then never pay you back"

⚓ THE DIVING CHALLENGE

Sometimes pirates can't just dig for treasure—they've got to swim for it. To prepare for undersea-treasure-diving, we've got a little game for you.

What you'll need for this challenge: Ten coins—pennies are fine, doubloons are preferred. The light attached to this book. A bed.

Here's how to do this challenge: Wait until it's nighttime and go into your room. Turn out the lights. It's pretty dark in there, isn't it? The only light on should be the one attached to this book. Now sit on your bed and throw the coins on the floor. Okay? Throw 'em overboard, *in the dark!*

Now you're going to use your light to go find the coins, but here's the snag: when you're off your bed, you have to try to hold your breath. Pretend your bed is your ship and the floor is underwater. If you feel like you can't hold it anymore, go back to your bed and take a breath.

Did you find all the coins? *(circle one)*
Yes / No / Maybe / It depends

If not, how many did you find? -

How many trips back to the bed did it take? - - - - - - - - - - - - - - - - -

Did you find anything else you've been looking for?
A nice scarf, perhaps?

Could you have done better? If you think you could have,

TRY AGAIN!

This time, did you find all the coins? *(circle one)*
Yes / No

If not, how many did you find? -

Once you've collected all the coins—every penny counts— you can turn to page 172 and check off COOK. Now go in the kitchen and make us some Parrot Pie, Cook. We're hungry for some talking bird!

ShArk SAFety

The best way to remain safe from shark attacks is to befriend the sharks. And the first step toward befriending them is to name them. Obvious, right? This is your **THIRTEENTH IMPORTANT LESSON**. Below are ten sharks. Name them! (Helpful hint: one of them is already named Irving. You just have to decide *which*.)

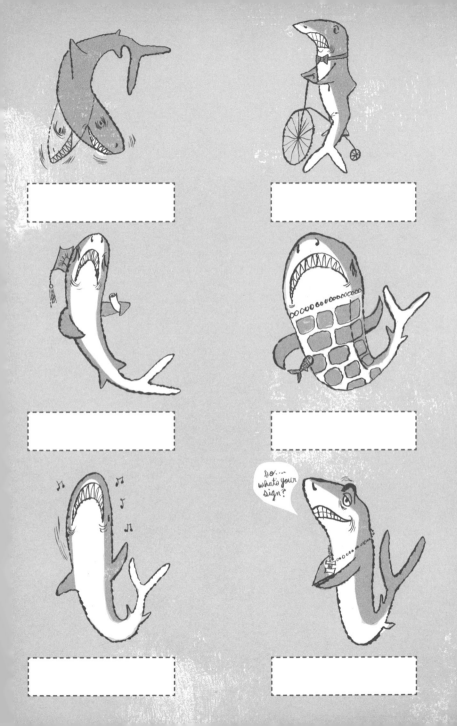

Here are the real names of those sharks. How can we be sure these are their names? Because we wrote this book, so we can say whatever we want. Check your answers written on the previous page to see if you named them correctly. (If you got them wrong, you probably could erase them and fix them up. In truth, we'd never know. Time and distance are separating us.)

THE FURY

IRVING THE-EATER-OF-PEOPLE-AND-THINGS

CLARABELLE FANCYFINGERS

NANCY THUNDERMAKER

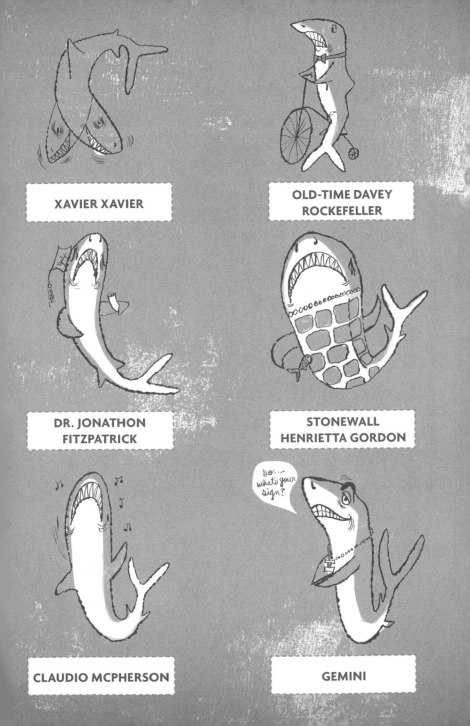

XAVIER XAVIER

OLD-TIME DAVEY ROCKEFELLER

DR. JONATHON FITZPATRICK

STONEWALL HENRIETTA GORDON

CLAUDIO MCPHERSON

GEMINI

PARROt TALK! PARROt TALK!

All good pirates have a parrot. It's a fact, at least as far as we know. Meet your new parrot, Oliver. He will be traveling with you wherever you go. In order to fully understand the parrot-pirate bond, you're going to have to get inside Oliver's head. Fill out the parrot's words in the following conversation. Remember: parrots can only repeat exactly what they've just heard.

Here we go:

PIRATE: "Arr, you're my best friend!"

PARROT: "Arr, you're my best friend!"

PIRATE: "Well thank you. That's nice to hear."

PARROT: ---

PIRATE: "I just said that."

PARROT: ---

PIRATE: "Stop copying me, you stupid bird!"

PARROT: ---

PIRATE: "I'm not a bird, you bird!"

PARROT: ---

PIRATE: "Who are you calling a bird, you bird?"

PARROT: ---

PIRATE: "I'm going to be having parrot stew if you keep that up."

PARROT: ---

PIRATE: "It's agreed. We'll both be eating parrot stew then!"

PARROT: ---

PIRATE: "I'm too old for this nonsense."

PARROT: ---

PIRATE: "Well then, I'll see you in the kitchen. I'll be wearing
my bib."

PARROT: ---

PIRATE: "You know your bib is at the cleaners'."

PARROT: ---

⚓ THE QUARTER-HUNT CHALLENGE, PART ONE

All pirates worth their weight in sea salt have something hidden somewhere. This is your **FOURTEENTH IMPORTANT LESSON**. Hiding things is just like putting them in a bank, but with more sand and fewer cameras. Everybody knows that the notorious Stabbin' Annie Goldwhiskers hid her keys so well that even she couldn't find them again! (Nobody knows, however, why she needed keys in the first place.)

You're going to start off your treasure collection with a quarter. That's what you'll be hiding first.

What you'll need for this challenge: Twenty-five cents. A place to dig. Something to dig with, like a spoon, a fork, a spork, or your "hook fingers"!

Here's how to do this challenge:
Step 1: Go get a quarter.
Step 2: Bury it nearby. Go do this right now. As always, we'll wait. (Here's us, waiting . . .)

WHOA, ARE YOU BACK ALREADY? That was quick. Okay, the next step will take place at night. We'll see you then.

Step 3: Is it nighttime already? Things sure move quickly in the pirate-book world. Okay, to make sure you don't forget where your quarter is, you should go get a piece of paper and draw a secret map of your quarter's location. It's so secret, in fact, that you'll need to draw your map under the covers, using the attached book light.

Important: Don't let anybody steal a look at your map. Otherwise, you may find yourself out a quarter.

Step 4: Once you've completed this map, roll it up and hide it in your sock drawer. We'll come back to this one later, but for right now, the map should be with the socks. (Please just trust us. When it comes to hiding things, we're total experts.)

Once you've stashed that map in your socks, you can turn to page 172 and put a check next to PEG-LEG-ATTACHER. Because that's what you are now! It's not a job to be taken lightly.

HOW TO DRAW PIRATE STUFF

Draw your own pirate here!

Add some extra stink-lines or seagulls or skeletons or
whatever you think will make him or her look really piratey.

⚓ THE MOST ANNOYING CHALLENGE IN THIS BOOK

Being on a ship for long periods of time means that every once in a while, you're going to end up talking about planks. It's just part of being a pirate. "Planks," someone will say. "Yeah," you'll say. "I'm glad you agree," they'll say. (Also, the scary idea of actually having to walk a plank into the deep, shark-infested ocean keeps people in their place.)

Today's challenge is to end every single conversation you have with the words **"You need to go walk the plank!"** Will this be confusing to just about everybody? It might. Will it startle people and keep them in their place? Perhaps. Will it be annoying to those who have to be around you all day?

Absolutely!

What you'll need for this challenge: Your voice. Some people to have conversations with. And those magically annoying seven words listed above.

Here's how to do this challenge: Start a conversation. Maybe say something like, "How's the weather up there?" Adults always think that's funny, especially if they're taller than you.

Chat with them for a while. Make it pleasant. In general, that's a good skill to have.

Now: When it feels like your conversation is starting to dwindle down a bit, this is the time to exclaim, "You need to go walk the plank!" Once you've done that, simply turn and walk briskly away. (If you're in class, go to the other side of the room.) See what happens! *Something?! Nothing?!*

At the end of the day, after having completed this challenge, fill out the following:

The most confused person I talked to was: _ _ _ _ _ _ _ _ _ _ _ _ _ _ _ _ _ _ _

The person who laughed the most was: _

The person who looked the most annoyed was: _ _ _ _ _ _ _ _ _ _ _ _ _ _

As long as your parents didn't throw away this book because you were so annoying today, you can go to page 72 and check off CANNON-LOADER. Keep up the good work, Cannon-Loader! You're getting closer to your very own captain's chair.

Did something unique occur with this challenge? Write us a letter and tell us about it. You can reach us at PirateLogContact@gmail.com.

A PiRAte RiDDLe

Here's a riddle:

"THE MORE YOU TAKE AWAY FROM ME, THE BIGGER I AM. IF YOU PUT ME IN A BARREL, IT WILL MAKE THE BARREL LIGHTER. WHAT AM I?"

Did you figure it out? The answer is: a hole. This is your **FIFTEENTH IMPORTANT LESSON**. The more dirt you take out of a hole, the bigger it gets. And if you make a hole in a barrel, everything will fall out and it'll get lighter. Pirates dig holes all the time. They dig holes when they're looking for treasure, and sometimes just when they're bored. How good are you at digging holes?

Draw yourself with a shovel
on the ground below:

OK, now draw yourself an hour
later after a whole lot of digging!

Nice digging! We just have one question, **CANNON-LOADER**.

HOW ARE YOU GOING TO GET OUT OF THERE?

⚓ THE ARRR CHALLENGE

Arrr is more than just a funny sound. It's a funny sound that captures the entire pirate way of life! As somebody probably said at some point, a good *Arrr* is worth a thousand other noises. But you can't expect yourself to deliver a first-class *Arrr* right away. No, no, no (no, no), no. Here are some exercises to get you to the peak of your *Arrr*-ability:

1. Make a very quiet *Arrr*.
2. Now a little louder.
3. A little bit louder.
4. Never mind if people are staring. We warned you about this. Keep on going. You're doing great.
5. Now, try making an *Arrr* as low and deep as you can.
6. This time, try it as squeaky and high as you can.
7. Say *Arrr* like it's a question. *Arrr?*
8. How long can you say *Arrr* without stopping for breath? Use a stopwatch and write down your best time here:
    ------ : ----------
9. Can you beat that time? Try again and write your new time here: ------ : ----------
10. Today, try to replace words like *yes* and *no* with *Arrr*. See if people can tell when you mean yes and when you mean no.

11. BONUS CHALLENGE: Replace all your words with *Arrr*.
    (Don't do this for too long. You could pull your *Arrr* muscle,
    and you'd have to wear a cast for a week.)

NICE ARRR-ING! After you complete this challenge, you can stop lugging around all those heavy cannonballs and turn to page 172. Change your status to FLAG-HOISTER. It's time to hoist some flags!

You've made some good progress, **FLAG-HOISTER**. It seems like you really do want to become a pirate. But if you want to keep going, you're going to need to make it official and fill out the paperwork for a Pirate's License. After all, if you're caught on the open sea without the required license, you can get into big trouble. To fill out the following forms and exams, you may have to flip back to previous pages in the book and even come up with some new stuff. But after you're done, you'll have a handy-dandy Pirate's License to keep forever!

PIRATE'S LICENSE FORMS

Your pirate name (see page 11):

_____

Your current ranking (see page 172):

_____

Age: _____

Height: _____

Hair color: _____

Beard color (this can be a future beard):

_____

Eye with eye patch: _____

Ship's name (see page 15): _____

Missing or loose limbs: _____

Breath (smelly or awful): _____

Favorite ice-cream flavor:

_____

Parrot's name:

_____

Parrot's height:

_____

Parrot's favorite ice-cream flavor (This is probably
just a copy of your answer. Parrots are such
copycats. And they really like ice cream. Especially
the kind of ice cream that you like. Do you like
vanilla? So do they. Unless you like chocolate.):

_____

The last time you ate some or all of a shark:

_____

The last time a shark ate some or all of you:

_____

Your bedtime: _____

(Trick question—pirates don't have bedtimes!)

Draw a picture of yourself here. If possible, make
it look menacing:

Pirate's License Exam, Page 1

You've got to talk the pirate-talk if you want to walk the pirate-walk (which is more of a hobble, but you already *knew* that). Let's find out how much pirate lingo you know. Below you'll find a list of pirate words with space to write the definitions. Even if you've never heard the word before, give it a guess. This exam will be graded on creativity, *not* on whether you get all the definitions "correct," so go ahead and make up some silly answers. Only after you're done should you flip the book over and read the *actual* definitions.

Pirate word #1: Cat-o'-nine-tails
What you think it means:_____

_____

_____

Pirate word #2: Cutlass
What you think it means:_____

_____

_____

Pirate word #3: **Forecastle**

What you think it means:_____

_____

_____

Pirate word #4: **Halyard**

What you think it means:_____

_____

_____

Pirate word #5: **Ketch**

What you think it means:_____

_____

_____

5. a small pirate boat
4. the rope used on pirate ships
3. the raised deck at the front of the ship
2. a short, wide sword
1. a whip made of nine strands of rope

93

Pirate's License Exam, Page 2

This is an exam in Pirate History. Circle whether you think each statement is true or false and then flip the book over to check your answers.

1. The world's first pirate was named Mickey Rooney.
   [] True
   [] False

2. Long John Silver's favorite weapon was a bag of squirrels, which he called Bag-o'-Nine-Squirrels.
   [] True
   [] False

3. When lost, pirates often navigate by their sense of taste.
   [] True
   [] False

4. Pirates invented Pop-Tarts.

   [] True

   [] False

5. The world's second pirate was named Andy Rooney.

   [] True

   [] False

6. None of the statements on this page are true.

   [] True

   [] False

hello there, again!

So you've made it through the first half of this book, which is mighty impressive. We think it's one of the most impressive things you've ever done, and that includes that one time you cleaned your room when you had that you-know-what growing under you-know-where. Remember that day? Nice cleaning!

Most readers of this book—and this is mainly true—fail at the Wooden-Leg Challenge, finding it difficult to hobble and wobble around all day and still concentrate on subtraction and social studies and stuff. But you did it!

We think that you're prepared for what's to come. (Or are you preparrrrrred? Or is that joke getting old?)

Anyway, we scored your exam and processed your paperwork, and we're happy to announce that you passed! Now you're allowed to fill out your pirate's license, which is required to sail high, medium, and low seas. NOTE: You must always have your license on you, whether in your wallet or pocket or eye patch.

This will come in handy when you tell somebody you're a pirate and they tell you to prove it. Here's one of those "prove it" conversations:

YOU: "I'm a pirate."
THEM: "Prove it."
YOU: (pulling out pirate license)
THEM: "Wow."
YOU: "I know."
THEM: (impressed)
YOU: (proud)

You're now officially a MATE on the ship! Go to page 172 and check it off!

See? So go ahead and fill this license out and then cut it out, remembering to add your pirate name, your ship's name, and so forth. Then turn the page and start your next adventure!

PIRATE'S LICENSE

INTN'L PIRATE ASSOCIATION

pirate name _____
ship's name _____
hair color _____
date of birth _____
eye patch over _____ eye

pirate signature

_____

PIRATE PHRASES

Now that you're a ship's Mate (and this is a big deal—don't kid yourself, kid), you've got to start talking like one. Add up these symbols to create pirate phrases!

Answers: 1. Jolly Roger 2. Walk the plank 3. Shiver me timbers 4. Land ho!

99

A LETTER HOME

Believe it or not, you've been at sea for two whole days now. Everybody at home is starting to miss you, the cute things you do, the funny things you say. Let's face it, **MATE**: you have a lot of good qualities, and you're an easy person to miss.

Also, before you shipped out, your exact words to everybody were, "Hey, everybody, after two days at sea, I'll write you a letter! I really will! Also, will you TiVo 'Dora the Explorer' for me?"

Anyway, you promised, and good pirates don't break their promises (unless there's a good reason). So now it's letter-writing time. Your task is to write a one-page letter detailing your experiences, including:

a. Whom you've *met* (think of other pirates who could be on board with you)
b. What you've *seen* (sea life? sea goose? Paris?)
c. Whether you've experienced any *danger* (maybe there was a storm; yes, let's say there was a storm)
d. What you have *found* so far
e. Whether you've had to walk any *planks*
f. What your current ranking is
g. Anything else you'd like to include

Remember to sign it using your pirate name!
We'll help you get started:

Dear _____ ,

It's been an amazing two days at sea! Listen to all this stuff
that's happened . . . _____
_____
_____
_____
_____
_____

Also, I met: _____
_____
_____
_____
_____

I saw: _____
_____
_____
_____
_____

I found: --

They call me: ----------------------------------

I can't wait to: --------------------------------

Your favorite pirate,

⚓ THE MESSAGE-IN-A-BOTTLE CHALLENGE

When you're in the middle of the ocean, it can be almost *impossible* to find a post office. And even if you do find one, who wants to wait in those horrible lines? Forget about it. That's what we say. And that's why the best choice for pirate communication is the message in a bottle!

Let's give it a shot, shall we?

What you'll need for this challenge: A soda bottle. A message.

Here's how to do this challenge: Get your letter. This could be the letter you wrote on the preceding page. (You wrote that, right? You didn't just skip ahead to this page? Because there's no cheating, **MATE,** especially when it comes to writing to people who miss you.) Or, if you prefer, it can be any other letter. It can even be a secret or a joke or a recipe or anything you want. It's just got to be on a piece of paper that you can roll up into a little tiny tube. Okay, write it down and then roll that sucker up.

Now get your soda bottle. Did you drink all the soda? If not, do that now. Or pour it all down the drain, which is the healthier alternative. Either way, there should be no more liquid in the bottle. Nobody wants a soggy letter. Okay, now stuff your rolled-up letter into the bottle and replace the cap.

HERE'S WHERE thiNGS GEt tRiCKY.

See, pirates would normally throw this message out into the sea, but you're on an *imaginary* ocean, **MATE**. If you just throw the bottle out your bedroom window, that's littering, and pirates don't litter, at least not in their own backyards. Instead, put your bottle in the recycling bin. You do recycle, don't you? Maybe someday somebody in a recycling plant will find your note and read it. Maybe not. The point of all of this is that you tried, **MATE**. You tried, and your message in a bottle is going on a journey without you . . .

Because you tried so hard, you have been promoted from Mate to FIRST MATE! Whoa! Go to page 172 to ch-ch-check it off.

RECORD YOUR DREAMS!

This is the section where you're going to record your nightly dreams. It will be interesting to see whether your dreams about pirates increase now that you're thinking about them so much and *becoming* one of them. Please do let us know if this happens. Best pirate wins.*

Regardless of what you dream about, though, write everything down, right when you wake up—using your book light if it's still dark outside or if you prefer to write your personal dreams under the covers—and see if you start to notice any patterns or meanings or special people or pirates popping up.

It'll be neat to have these in a few years!

Date: _____

Last night I dreamed about: _____
_____
_____

I also dreamed about: _____
_____
_____

* Not an actual contest.

Date: --

Last night I dreamed about: ------------------------------------
----

I also dreamed about: ---

Date: --

Last night I dreamed about: ------------------------------------
----

I also dreamed about: ---

Date: _____

Last night I dreamed about: _____
_____
_____

I also dreamed about: _____
_____
_____

Date: _____

Last night I dreamed about: _____
_____
_____

I also dreamed about: _____
_____
_____

IN CASE OF EMERGENCY

Surely you know that all pirates need an escape plan, a way
to save themselves when the going gets a little rougher
than they were hoping for. If you didn't know this, it's your
SIXTEENTH IMPORTANT LESSON.

What if something goes seriously wrong and you're just sort
of sitting there and everybody is really busy saving themselves
and you're like, "Hey guys?" and they're not paying attention to
your questions? What then?

Or maybe they're like, "Run!" and you're like, "Run *where*?
And they're all like, "You should *know* this already!"

That's why you're going to make an "In Case of Emergency"
chart. Fill in the blanks with the appropriate responses.

In case of a minor ship emergency, I will _____
_____
_____

In case of a major ship emergency, I will _____
_____
_____

In case of iceberg, I will _____
_____
_____

If another ship attacks us, I will _____
_____
_____

In case of cannonball flying through the air, about to crash into
us, I will _____
_____
_____

If really big waves crash aboard the ship, I will
_____
_____

In case of a bad hair day, I will _____
_____
_____

If a shark somehow flops aboard, I will _____
_____
_____

If a fire starts, I will _____

_____

_____

In case of an outbreak of pinkeye, I will _____

_____

_____

If a shark with pinkeye flops aboard and starts lighting fires
everywhere, I will _____

_____

_____

If my friend turns out to be my enemy, I will _____

_____

_____

If my enemy turns out to be my cousin, I will _____

_____

_____

If my cousin turns out to be my friend, I will _____

_____

_____

⚓ THE QUARTER-HUNT CHALLENGE, PART TWO

Remember that quarter you hid a while ago, outside somewhere? And remember how you drew a map to find the quarter, and then you hid the map in your sock drawer? We were all so much younger then . . .

Here's the next part of that challenge: You are going to take the map out of your sock drawer and hide it somewhere else. Then you'll create a clue that has instructions for finding that map. This way, if somebody reads the clue and finds the map, they can use the map to track down that shiny quarter. We realize that this is one of the more complex challenges, so you'll have to pay close attention.

What you'll need for this challenge: A code that will involve spelling words backward! A place to hide the code.

Here's how to do this challenge: Grab that first map you drew—the one that says how to find your quarter. Take it out of your sock drawer. Go and hide that map in an awesome, super-secret, maptastic spot. Maybe on a bookshelf between some books? Maybe in a flowerpot between some flowers? **GO! NOW!** (We'll wait. Here's us waiting . . .)

DANG, YOU'RE BACK ALREADY? You're very quick. Okay, now you're going to make a clue to help somebody in the future find your hidden map. Go get a new piece of paper and a pencil. All you have to do is write where you hid the map with the letters backward. Get it?

So if you went and hid your first map in the fridge, you should write "fridge" backward on your newest clue: **E-G-D-I-R-F**

If you hid it in your pants drawer, write:
R-E-W-A-R-D S-T-N-A-P
(NOTE: We just realized that *drawer* spelled backward is *reward*, which is much more satisfying than *fridge* spelled backward being *egdirf*. What's an egdirf, anyway? If you know, please write and tell us.) Best egdirf definition wins.*

Once you create this code, you should hide this newest clue in your sock drawer and wait for further instructions.

First Mate, you're doing a great job. Because you did such good work on this challenge, you've been promoted to QUARTERMASTER. Go to page 172 to add a check next to your new rank.

* Not an actual contest.

HAR HAR HAR!

You probably already know this, **QUARTERMASTER**, but pirates are not good at telling jokes. In fact, they are downright terrible. Here are a few jokes invented by pirates:

Q: Why did the pirate cross the road?
A: Because she felt like it! Arrrrrrrrrrrrrrrrrr!

Q: How many pirates does it take to change a lightbulb?
A: Lightbulbs don't exist yet! Arrrrrrrrrrrrrrrr!

Q: What's the opposite of the word *aren't*?
A: The word *arrrrrrrrrrrrrrrrrrrr*.

Q: What comes after the letter Q in the alphabet?
A: The letter *arrrrrrrrrrrrrrrrrrrrrr*.

You see? Just terrible. Fortunately, you're here now. And it's joke time. And you've brought your sense of humor, which we've heard so much about.

We're going to set you up with a few questions or answers, and all you have to do is fill in the blanks with some of your own hilarious words. If you think your jokes are particularly good, you should send them to us at PirateLogContact@gmail.com.

Q: Why did the pirate cross the road?
A: _____

Q: How many pirates does it take to change a lightbulb?
A: _____

Q: _____
A: Because he saw a shark behind him!

SEND THEM TO US!

IMPORTANT ANNOUNCEMENT! The ship's too heavy and they're getting rid of any unnecessary cargo. You'll actually have to walk the plank unless you can explain why you'd make a great pirate and why you're important to this ship. Are you very clever? Do you have incredible skills with a sword? Can you cook? All of these things might help. Unfortunately, you can't use any of those examples, because *we* thought of them. Get your own. **YOUR TURN!**

List ten things that make you a valuable addition to the ship. If you can come up with ten, then it's okay to stay on board and continue to the next challenge.

1. _____

_____

2. _____

_____

3. _____

_____

4. _____

_____

5. ---

----

6. ---

----

7. ---

----

8. ---

----

9. ---

----

10. ---

Some of the other pirates on board couldn't think of ten things
and were cast off. But you made it.

CONGRATULATIONS!

⚓ THE STUFF-HIDING CHALLENGE

Hiding your stuff well is key if you don't want people finding it. This is your **SEVENTEENTH IMPORTANT LESSON**.

What you'll need for this challenge: The light attached to this book. Ten small (inexpensive) objects from your house. This could include toothpaste or a cup or some silverware or the shampoo. We think items from the kitchen or bathroom work well. (But don't take everything from the same place, or it'll be too obvious! And don't take anything that can rot if it's not found. Hiding cheese is never a good idea, especially when there's a chance of being grounded.)

Here's how to do this challenge: At night, when the lights are out and people are in bed and the house is quiet, take this collection of useful stuff and—guided by your book light—find some neat hiding places for it.

Hiding places could include: behind a book; under a table; beneath the couch; in some random drawer; beneath the dog; under the cat; behind the bird; in the refrigerator, etc., etc.

To be fair, hide the stuff in a place where it actually might be found if somebody took the trouble to look. Don't put it in a sock and then put that sock inside of another sock and then put that sock . . . well, you get the idea.

Eventually, people in your house might start to ask about this stuff. Keep track of who said what here. Also, keep a tally of the number of days that the stuff remains hidden.

Try to keep everything hidden for a week. If a week passes and the toothpaste is still secure in its original hiding place, quietly (again, using your light) place the stuff back where you found it. You have succeeded in this challenge!

If people start finding the stuff, though, you might need to work a little bit on your hiding skills. Repeat entire challenge if necessary.

The stuff you hid: _____

_____

_____

_____

_____

_____

_____

Who said what about the missing stuff: -

- -

- -

- -

- -

- -

The number of days each object remained hidden: - - - - - - - - - - -

- -

- -

- -

- -

- -

What was found, if anything: -

- -

- -

- -

- -

Once you've completed this challenge, you can go to page 172 and check the box next to OFFICER. You're getting to be pretty big time!

PIRATE TREASURE MAZE!

Start at your ship and work your way toward the treasure chest.

take the wheel

The captain's been steering the boat for four days straight, **OFFICER**. He's getting cranky and he needs a nap, so you'll have to take the wheel for a couple of minutes. If you can guide the ship through these dangerous waters, you'll get the treasure waiting on the other side.

make a choice

You are on a remote, overgrown island with two of your shipmates, a couple of shady characters you wouldn't trust with a nickel, let alone a dime. They'd watch your back in a fight, but they'd take your wallet in a pinch.

This is the first time you've been to this particular island, and you're walking the shore together, investigating your surroundings. You don't see much . . . maybe a few trees . . . some sand . . . a few more trees . . . until . . . at the exact same moment!! . . . gleaming in the sandy distance . . . wait for it . . . are you ready? . . . *at the exact same moment,* the three of you spot three treasure chests! **WHAT ARE THE ODDS?** Three pirates and three treasure chests in the sand? Perhaps—in the history of time and the history of treasure and the history of finding things—this has never happened before. It's truly a big deal, and for a split second, you're lost in the moment. "Wow," you think. "Neat," you say. Then you remember who you're standing next to, the scum that they are, the things that they want. "Grr," they respond. Or maybe it's somebody's hungry stomach responding. Really, it doesn't matter.

Somebody's going to have to make a move. You're going to have to make a decision, and you're only going to get one shot to put your arms around the treasure chest of your choice. Based on what you see and your worldly pirate instincts, you need to pick a treasure chest.

QUICKLY!

(Remember: In life, there are occasions when there are no wrong answers. This is not one of those occasions. Here, now, there are at least two wrong answers. And no cheating by skipping ahead, because that makes you as bad as the rest of these guys, and who wants to think that about himself or herself?) Circle the chest you choose. After you circle your chest, turn to page 165 to see what else you get!

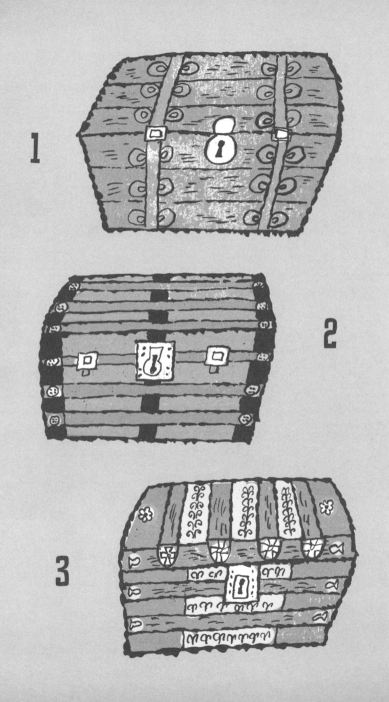

StRange But tRue!

We know this page will seem unrelated to the rest of this journal, but—as a pirate—it's the **EIGHTEENTH IMPORTANT LESSON** for you to know: All fish, everywhere, have a favorite movie on DVD. Weird, right? But true. It's very true.

Draw lines to match each fish on the left with the movie of its choice on the right. The answer key's on the next page.

BIG-MOUTH BASS

RAINBOW TROUT

ANCHOVY

CLOWN FISH

ANGLER

ELECTRIC EEL

ABOUT A BOY

THE ROYAL TENENBAUMS

FINDING NEMO

FOUR WEDDINGS & A FUNERAL

THE EMPIRE STRIKES BACK

SCROOGED

COMPLIMENT-the-CAPTAIN DAY!

Remember this, **OFFICER**: One of the best ways to get ahead as a pirate is flattery—saying nice things, even if you don't necessarily mean them. Here's your captain. Find ten nice things to say about him. We'll get you started:

1. Hey. Nice boots.

2. Your teeth are less yellow than yesterday.

3. _____
   _____

4. _____
   _____

5. _____
   _____

6. _____
   _____

7. _____

_____

8. _____

_____

9. _____

_____

10. _____

_____

WhiRLPOOLeD!

Imagine this: You're sailing along and everything is peaceful, the sun is setting, and you're just about to sit down for dinner. Everything seems right. You sigh. "Finally," you think to yourself, "a calm night. And boy am I hungry."

And then all of a sudden, your boat is trapped in a whirlpool, everything is spinning, your dinner quickly flies overboard, people are hollering, nobody knows what the heck to do or where the heck to go. **SEASICKNESS ABOUNDS!**

Use this whirlpool-shape line to write about what you will do next and how you will help your ship.

WHEN MY SHIP WAS CAUGHT IN A WHIRLPOOL, HERE'S HOW I HELPED:

WE WANT YOU!

Sometimes it's hard to get enough pirates on the ship. After all, it's a tough job, everybody smells, and there's always a chance that your ship will suddenly veer into a whirlpool. **YIKES**.

The captain has asked you to do a little bit of public relations for your vessel, to make sure that it's well staffed on your next outing.

You're going to create a billboard (right) that will hang near the water (or on your door), so potential pirates will be able to decide whether they want to come with you.

Make sure to draw a picture showing some sort of adventure that you will have. (You also might want to make sure that the people in your drawing seem to be having fun!)

In addition to the drawing, you'll want to have a motto—something that's catchy and will make people want to be a part of your crew.

Sample mottos:

1. "You've always wanted to be a pirate—now's the time!"
2. "Looking for an adventure?"
3. "You're not doing anything with your life, anyway!"

After you create your billboard, cut it out and hang it on your bedroom door. Find out how many people want to join your cause.

The captain will be very happy with you once you have a big crew again. And if you do your job right, **OFFICER**, you will.

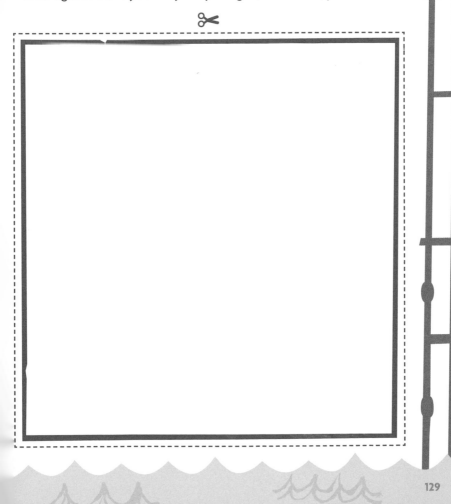

ChickeN SOUP FOR the PiRAte SOUL

Pirates are a hungry lot and will eat just about anything.

Here are some ingredients you can always find on a ship: fish, crackers, flour, water, chickens, eggs, limes, and rats. What can you make out of all this? Make up a dish and describe it, so your fellow pirates will want to eat some.

The title of your dish: _____

_____

The ingredients that you'll use: _____

_____

_____

_____

_____

Describe this dish for people who have never heard of it:

_____

_____

_____

_____

_____

Rhyme time

As we've said, pirates are clever folks. They're ready to make up songs about the sea on the spot. The sea-spot. These are a special type of song called sea chanteys. And the first step in making up a sea chantey is being able to rhyme. We want you to time yourself as you come up with at least five rhymes for each of these words:

(EASY WORDS)

Sea (for example, "bee")

1. ------------------------
2. ------------------------
3. ------------------------
4. ------------------------
5. ------------------------

TIME ------ : ------------

Gold

1. ------------------------
2. ------------------------
3. ------------------------
4. ------------------------
5. ------------------------

TIME ------ : ------------

Ship

1. ------------------------
2. ------------------------
3. ------------------------
4. ------------------------
5. ------------------------

TIME ------ : ------------

Hook

1. ------------------------
2. ------------------------
3. ------------------------
4. ------------------------
5. ------------------------

TIME ------ : ------------

Leg

1. _____
2. _____
3. _____
4. _____
5. _____
TIME _____ : _____

Shark

1. _____
2. _____
3. _____
4. _____
5. _____
TIME _____ : _____

(HARDER WORDS)

Lieutenant

1. _____
2. _____
3. _____
4. _____
5. _____
TIME _____ : _____

Eye patch

1. _____
2. _____
3. _____
4. _____
5. _____
TIME _____ : _____

Silver

1. _____
2. _____
3. _____
4. _____
5. _____
TIME _____ : _____

Swashbuckler

1. _____
2. _____
3. _____
4. _____
5. _____
TIME _____ : _____

⚓ THE ARRRR-IN-THE-CARRRR CHALLENGE

As we've already mentioned, every pirate worth his or her weight in seawater wears an eye patch most of the time. What's also common knowledge is every pirate worth his or her weight in "arrr"s (which are much harder to measure) regularly says "Arrr." This is truth. This is your **NINETEENTH IMPORTANT LESSON**.

Today, you're going to combine these two vital elements (patches and "arrrr"s) for another fun-filled physical challenge.

What you'll need for this challenge: An eye patch, or at least something that will cover up one eye and look stylish at the same time. A ride in a car on a road where there's traffic. A driver.

What you shouldn't do: Drive the car yourself.

Here's why: Because it's harder to measure depth with one eye covered up.

And also: You're not old enough to drive yet, right?

Here's how to do this challenge: Are you in the car yet? We'll wait. You there? Okay, good. Put on the patch. Nice and snug? You can check the mirror, but your eye patch might be closer than it appears.

Ask the driver to start driving. Make sure your window is down. As you pull up next to cars at stoplights and stop signs—or even when you pass them on the street—yell your most convincing "Arrr!!!" See how many people "arrr" right back at you.

Keep a tally below of the "arrr"s you get in return. Try to get at least ten. Or way more.

Number of people you "arrr"ed at: _____
Number of people who "arrr"ed back: _____
Number of people who simply stared: _____

NICE WORK TODAY,
Officer. Hopefully, you arrr'd at a lot of people. As a reward, you can turn to page 172 and check off BOATSWAIN. What does a boatswain do? We don't know exactly. But it's a neat title and it's better than Shark-Bait—that's for sure!

thINK FAST!

There's a giant wave approaching! Decide what these pirates have to say about it! Are they scared? Excited? Bored? It's all up to you. Add words to the bubbles provided.

HOW to DRAW PiRAte StuFF

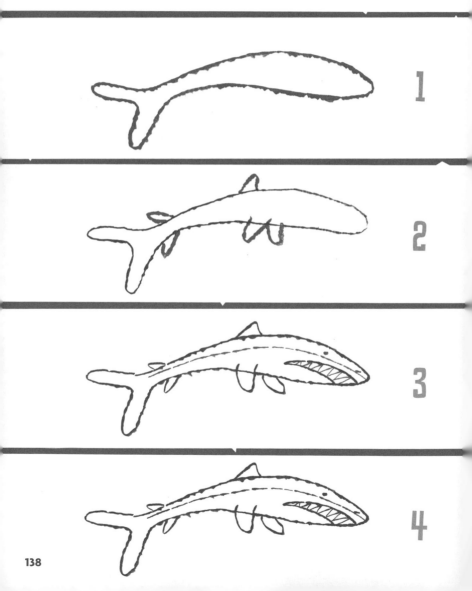

1

2

3

4

Draw your own shark here!

Add some extra teeth or fins or stink lines
or robot armor—whatever you like!

ShARK VS. SQUiD

It's always worth asking: Which sea creature would win in a fight, a **GIANT SQUID** or a **GREAT WHITE SHARK**?

Before you write your answer, here are a few details to help you make your decision:

- **THE SQUID TOOK KARATE CLASSES FROM AGES SIX TO EIGHT.**
- **THE SHARK IS MISSING ALL BUT ONE OF ITS TEETH.**
- **THE SQUID HAS JUST COME FROM A LOSING BATTLE WITH A DIFFERENT SHARK.**
- **THAT SINGLE SHARK TOOTH THAT WE MENTIONED HAS THE ABILITY TO SHOOT FIREBALLS (DON'T ASK).**
- **THE SQUID IS COLOR-BLIND.**

Who would win? *(circle one)*

The giant squid / The great white shark

Tell us why: _____

_____

_____

Your crew was out swimming and is suddenly surrounded by sharks! **LOTS OF SHARKS!** Sharks that haven't eaten in a while. Also, they really, really like blood. To make matters worse, your buddy Carl just skinned his knee on the diving plank. This is getting very, very dangerous. What does your crew have to say about it? Add their words to the bubbles provided!

⚓ THE SECRET-HANDSHAKE CHALLENGE

It's important to know who's on your side at all times. As the old sea-saying goes, "You don't want to turn your back on the pirate who's going to push you overboard into the ocean and laugh heartily as he sails into the distance and you're just floating there in the ocean with a bunch of sharks and whales and other scary stuff below you."

It's a famous old saying. Look it up if you don't believe us.

The best way to quickly establish who's on your side and who's an enemy bent on stealing your stuff and pushing you overboard is with a secret handshake (or hook-shake, if you're lacking in hands).

What you'll need for this challenge: Your hand. And somebody else's hand.

Or: Your hook. And somebody else's hook.

Here's how to do this challenge: This is where you get creative. You need to come up with at least three "moves" that will be part of your hand-hook-shake. But more is better!

Maybe your index finger scratches the inside of somebody's palm. Maybe you and your partner slap the backs of your hands together first. With two hands or hooks and some free time, there are infinite possibilities for making your shake one of the hardest codes to crack on the sea. NOTE: This is a **SECRET** handshake, which means that not a lot of people should know about it.

Describe your secret handshake here:

First, we will _____.

_____

Then, we _____.

_____

Next, we _____.

_____

Keep adding moves here, if you come up with more than three:

_____

_____

You can teach your handshake to ten people. Eleven, tops. Don't let anybody else know about it, or else it won't be a secret shake anymore!

As long as you keep your handshake a secret and tell only your closest, piratiest friends, you can advance from Boatswain to MASTER! You're getting real close! Remember when you were just a Spit-Scrubber? Ah, memories.

HOW tO DRAW PiRAte StuFF

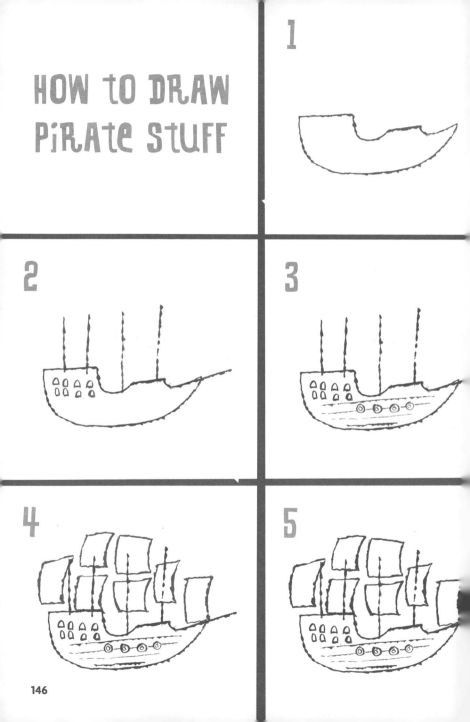

Draw your pirate ship here!

If you want, draw yourself on board, steering. Watch out for that iceberg! Just kidding! Or are we? Sometimes it's hard to tell. As always, any stink lines that you draw will be an excellent addition.

ANOTHER LETTER HOME

You've been at sea for a little over two weeks. You're starting to miss your favorite foods. Write a letter home, asking for a care package that has some of this food in it.

Dear --,

I loved it when you used to make: ------------------------

Here's why: --

Your favorite pirate,

----

excuses, excuses

You had a bunch of chores to do today, but you didn't get around to a couple of them, and now the captain wants to know why. We'll give you a couple of possible excuses; you pick the one that sounds the best.

1. Why didn't you swab the deck?
   - ☐ a. "It's my birthday. Leave me alone."
   - ☐ b. "Look over there!" (Run away.)
   - ☐ c. "I don't know what 'swab' means."

2. Why didn't you raise the sails?
   - ☐ a. "My arms were tired. I've been shark wrestling."
   - ☐ b. "I did. Look over there!" (Run away, giggling.)
   - ☐ c. "I thought you said 'whales.' That's why there's a gigantic whale at the top of the ship's mast. Because I thought that's what you wanted. I spent all day getting that thing up there. That's one heavy dude."

3. Why didn't you polish the swords?
   - ☐ a. "I'm allergic to swords."
   - ☐ b. "My alarm didn't go off."
   - ☐ c. "I was busy swabbing the deck."

4. Why didn't you cook the grub?

☐ a. "The guys in the kitchen smell funny."

☐ b. "I'm allergic to grub and it's my birthday and my alarm didn't go off."

☐ c. "I don't like your tone of voice."

5. Why didn't you walk the sea dog?

☐ a. "I'm allergic to sea dogs."

☐ b. "I'm more of a sea cat person."

☐ c. "I'm allergic to sea cats."

See the bottom of the next page for the answers.

FIG. 1

UNDERSEA DISCOVERY!

You have been forced to walk the plank because there was some slime found on one of the dishes, and sometimes you're the dishwasher. There is **NO** getting out of the plank-walking. You walk it (see fig. 1) and you splash deeeeeeeeeeeeeeeep into the cold and salty ocean. While underwater, you see something that no one will believe. Everybody will be sooooooooooo impressed by what you found. Wow. It's just amazing. Seriously. Write about what you see: _____

_____

_____

_____

_____

_____

_____

_____

_____

_____

_____

_____

_____

_____

SiNG YOUR PiRAte HeARt OUt

Songs are a very important part of life at sea. This is your
TWENTIETH IMPORTANT LESSON.

It's necessary to keep spirits high during the long and difficult
days of pillaging and looting. Singing is one of the best ways to
do that.

We'd like you to create an original sea chantey, something that's
never been heard or sung before. When you're finished, send
your chanteys to us at PirateLogContact@gmail.com. We will
take our favorites, record them with our own pirate band, and
post them on the Web, giving you full credit for your efforts.

For your original sea chantey, go ahead and use your rhyming
words from page 132. This will make everything so easy!

Examples of things to sing about:
- **THE WAVES**
- **THE SHIP**
- **SAILING**
- **BEING BETTER THAN EVERYBODY ELSE**

- **BEING RICHER THAN EVERYBODY ELSE**
- **BEING SMARTER AND BETTER AND RICHER THAN EVERYBODY ELSE**
- **SHARKS**

Write your song here: ----------------------------------

----

tattoos are forever

Your shipmate really wants a tattoo. She'll probably regret it in a little bit, but she wants it now. She knows you're creative, so she's coming to you for advice. Come up with five original ideas for tattoos. Draw them or describe them in words here:

tReASUReI

Your ship has found treasure. Congratulations! You will get fifty gold coins to spend as you wish. You have to spend it all now, so pick items that add up to your total. Circle the items you want:

a. Sword: Ten coins

b. Gold-plated eye patch: Twelve coins

c. Super-intelligent parrot: Two and a half coins

d. Lard: Twenty coins

e. Moose eggs: Six coins

f. One hundred fifty berries (various): Two coins

g. Super-plank: Eight coins

h. Ice-cream bar: Twenty coins

i. Treasure map: Free with purchase of moose eggs

j. Thirty coins: Five coins

k. The ability to see sound: Fifteen coins

l. A dog that can write: Nineteen coins

m. Bacon bits: One coin

n. Ant farm: Eleven coins

o. Lucky underpants: Nineteen coins

p. A nice bandana: Two coins

q. An ugly bandana: Three coins

How many gold coins did you spend? _____

⚓ THE FINAL QUARTER-HUNT CHALLENGE

Remember alllllllllll the way back to those innocent days when you were outside burying a quarter? Those were good days, huh?

And then remember creating a map that showed where the quarter was buried? And then you hid that map in your sock drawer for a while, but then we asked you to hide it somewhere else? And then you created a backward code to find the map? And then you hid the code sheet? Remember all that?

GOSH, this is getting complicated.

Here, now, finally, is the final part of this entire deal.

What you'll need for this challenge: A poem, which you will write on the next page. A friend or family member to go on a quarter-hunt.

Here's how to do this challenge: Take the instructions with the backward-code sheet out of your sock drawer and find a good hiding place for it. **GO! NOW!** (As always, we'll wait! We're waiting!)

Now here's what you need to do next: Create a rhyming poem that tells people where the backward-code sheet is hidden.

Here's an example (which you shouldn't use, because we wrote it and we want you to write your own). If you hid your clue behind a dictionary, you could write a poem like this:

**IF YOU'RE WONDERING WHERE TO LOOK,
YOU MIGHT START BEHIND THIS BOOK.
IF YOU LOOK INSIDE, YOU'LL SEE
EVERY WORD FROM A TO Z!**

Your poem goes here: _____
_____
_____
_____
_____
_____
_____
_____
_____

Once you create your rhyming poem, find somebody to show it to. He or she should have all the information needed to track down the code sheet, the map, and the quarter!

The rhyming poem should lead to the code, which should lead to the map, which should lead to the quarter!

Whew!

What was the hardest part of this challenge for you? _ _ _ _ _ _ _ _ _
_ _
_ _
_ _
_ _
_ _

What was the hardest part of this challenge for the person looking for the code, the map, and the quarter? _ _ _ _ _ _ _ _ _ _ _ _ _
_ _
_ _
_ _
_ _
_ _

Was the quarter eventually found? *(circle one)*

yes / no

Did somebody else dig up the quarter before
you could get to it? *(circle one)*

yes / no

If you had the chance to do it all over again, would you hide
the stuff somewhere else? If so, where? _____

_____

_____

_____

_____

WOW. What a relief to finally dig up
that quarter again and be done with this
challenge, definitely the most involved
one in the book. All those clues were so
complicated. But you did it. And because
you did such a good job, we're promoting
you to LIEUTENANT. That's only one rank
below Captain! Amazing!

CONCLUSiON

(NOTE: For full and total effect, this page is to be read after you have completed all the activities in this book.)

You are a pirate. In fact, you are a very good pirate. We know this. You have proven yourself time and time again, by making maps and writing sea chanteys, walking with a limp and "arr"ing at people through your car window. You have hidden and found quarters, prevented scurvy, written with hook-fingers, designed an escape plan, written pirate movie reviews, and designed a billboard to recruit for your ship.

You have given yourself a new name, gone unshaven and unbathed, created seawater, designed new constellations, conversed with a parrot, found treasure and—through the completion of every physical challenge—progressed up the ranking chart until you found yourself here and now, **LIEUTENANT**.

Your **TWENTY-FIRST IMPORTANT LESSON** is that hard work pays off. You have done everything we've asked of you and more. An incredible amount of complicated stuff had to happen for you to reach this point. You've gone through plenty of changes, and we salute you. But your journey is not over. Oh no.

IN FACT, the MOST iMPORTANT PARt OF YOUR jOURNeY iS juSt beGiNNiNG.

Without doing anything more (this promotion is on us), turn the page and fill out your final certificate,

CAPTAIN.

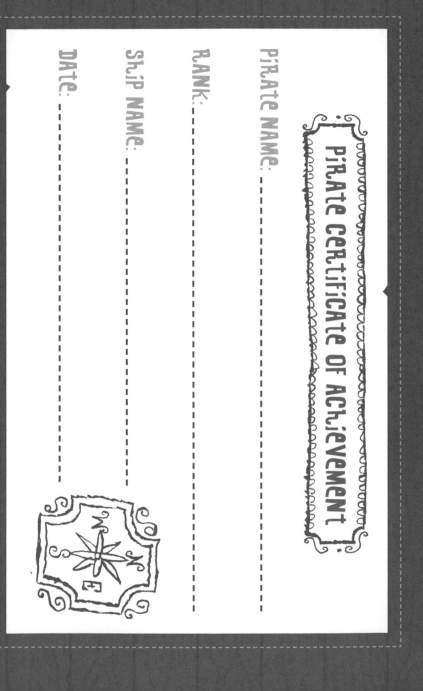

PiRATe CERTiFiCATE OF ACHieVeMeNT

PiRATe NAME: - - - - - - - - - - - - - -

RANK: - - - - - - - - - - - - - -

SHiP NAME: - - - - - - - - - - - - - -

DATE: - - - - - - - - - - - - - -

WhiCh ChESt DiD yOU ChOOSe (See Pg. 123)?

Read on to see what you've won:

CHOOSE YOUR TREASURE CHEST OPtION 1

If you chose Treasure Chest #1, congratulations! Inside are: a jetpack, fifty-five gold coins, a shoe that's also a working telephone, a monkey that can do backflips, three much smaller treasure chests, two copies of this journal, a stapler, a broken remote control, a cup of tea (cold), a dirty plastic bag full of paper clips, and a waffle.

CHOOSE YOUR TREASURE CHEST OPtION 2

If you chose Treasure Chest #2, congratulations! Inside are: two unicorns (stuffed), a time machine (real), twenty chocolate bars (no walnuts), three spoons and a roll of toilet paper, and a DVD box set of *The Golden Girls* (unable to play the special features, because there's a scratch).

CHOOSE YOUR TREASURE CHEST OPtION 3

If you chose Treasure Chest #3, congratulations! Inside are: an invisibility suit, a crystal ball, two friendly dinosaurs, the bounciest rubber ball in the world, one unfriendly dinosaur, and a talking bike. Plus everything that is in Chests #1 and #2. Chest #3 is the best choice.

Reference Section

Pirate Measurement Conversion

(NOTE: All figures are estimates)

3 daggers = 1 sword

18 tiny pirates = 3 large pirates

2 tablespoons of lard = 1 gold coin

2 huge pirate ships = 3 large ships

13 red pirate hats = 12 ½ blue pirate hats

2 eye patches = 0 good eyes

1 peg leg = ¹⁄₁₀₀₀ former tree

1 case of scurvy = 26 cases of head lice

26 cases of head lice = 3 daggers

Data on Legs Lost / Peg Legs Sold (1962–1966)

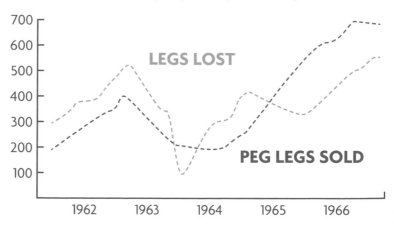

Official Pirate Holidays

1. International Talk Like a Pirate Pirate Day — September 19

And that's it. There are no more yet. But with your help, we can change that. Maybe October 3 could be Scurvy Awareness Day. Or July 10 could be Parrot Appreciation Day. In a perfect world, every day would be a pirate day! Think about it: more pirate holidays mean more pirate presents and more pirate-shaped cakes. Everybody likes cake. And that's your **TWENTY-SECOND IMPORTANT LESSON**.

Here's some room to write your ideas for pirate-related holidays: _____
_____
_____

Here's what you can do to help: Make up a couple of pirate holidays, then get a bunch of your friends to sign the petition on the next page. Try to get so many signatures that you have to get another page for them. Once you feel like you've got enough, send them to a senator or a celebrity or somebody who seems like they might be in charge. When they see how many signatures you've got, we bet they'll seriously consider making more pirate holidays. And then, bam! Pirate-shaped cake for everyone. We'll all have you to thank. **NICE JOB!**

PETITION FOR PIRATE HOLIDAYS

VeRy iMPORtANt PiRAte LessONs

FIRST IMPORTANT LESSON: Pirates don't care who's looking.

SECOND IMPORTANT LESSON: Make stuff up.

THIRD IMPORTANT LESSON: Never bring more than ten things on a pirate ship.

FOURTH IMPORTANT LESSON: The most important skill on a pirate ship is knot-tying.

FIFTH IMPORTANT LESSON: Every pirate who's any pirate wears a patch over at least one of his or her eyes, most of the time.

SIXTH IMPORTANT LESSON: You have to earn your eye patch.

SEVENTH IMPORTANT LESSON: You should avoid scurvy at all costs.

EIGHTH IMPORTANT LESSON: A lot of pirates have hooks because, one way or another they lost a hand or two or—much more rarely—three. It's just another part of daily life at sea.

NINTH IMPORTANT LESSON: It's tremendously hard to shave when you're out at sea.

TENTH IMPORTANT LESSON: Bathing is for landlubbers.

ELEVENTH IMPORTANT LESSON: The peg leg is an acceptable replacement for the foot, but it'll never be quite the same.

TWELFTH IMPORTANT LESSON: Pirates spend most of their lives on boats, so they have to get used to seasickness.

THIRTEENTH IMPORTANT LESSON: The best way to remain safe from shark attacks is to befriend the sharks. And the first step toward befriending them is to name them.

FOURTEENTH IMPORTANT LESSON: All pirates have something hidden somewhere.

FIFTEENTH IMPORTANT LESSON: The more you take out of a hole, the bigger it gets.

SIXTEENTH IMPORTANT LESSON: All pirates need an escape plan.

SEVENTEENTH IMPORTANT LESSON: Hiding your stuff well is key if you don't want people finding it.

EIGHTEENTH IMPORTANT LESSON: All fish, everywhere, have a favorite movie on DVD.

NINETEENTH IMPORTANT LESSON: Every pirate worth his or her weight in "arrr"s regularly says "Arrr."

TWENTIETH IMPORTANT LESSON: Songs are a very important part of life at sea.

TWENTY-FIRST IMPORTANT LESSON: Hard work pays off.

TWENTY-SECOND IMPORTANT LESSON: Everybody likes cake.

TWENTY-THIRD IMPORTANT LESSON: Never trust an important lesson in a pirate book.

RANKINGS:

(Check these off when we tell you to)

- ☐ **SHARK-BAIT**
- ☐ **LANDLUBBER**
- ☐ **SQUID-KISSER**
- ☐ **PARROT-TRAINER**
- ☐ **SPIT-SCRUBBER**
- ☐ **MOP-CARRIER**
- ☐ **SAILMAKER**
- ☐ **DECK-SWABBER**
- ☐ **HOOK-SHARPENER**
- ☐ **CARPENTER**
- ☐ **COOK**

- ☐ **PEG-LEG-ATTACHER**
- ☐ **CANNON-LOADER**
- ☐ **FLAG-HOISTER**
- ☐ **MATE**
- ☐ **FIRST MATE**
- ☐ **QUARTERMASTER**
- ☐ **OFFICER**
- ☐ **BOATSWAIN**
- ☐ **MASTER**
- ☐ **LIEUTENANT**
- ☐ **CAPTAIN**